This book belongs to:

____

18549240R00069

Made in the USA
San Bernardino, CA
20 December 2018